Beginner's Guide to Keeping Venomous Snakes

by Lenny Flank, Jr

Red and Black Publishers, St Petersburg, Florida

NOTE: Snake handling is *extremely dangerous*. This book is presented for *informational purposes* only. *It is not intended to serve as a course or instruction in the art of handling venomous snakes.* It is *impossible* to learn how to safely handle venomous snakes from a book. If you want to learn how to safely handle venomous snakes, find an experienced snake handler who can give you practical hands-on training. And *if you don't know what you are doing, don't try anything you see in this book*. Don't be stupid.

Library of Congress Cataloging-in-Publication Data

Flank, Lenny.
  Beginner's guide to keeping venomous snakes / by Lenny Flank, Jr.
      p. cm.
  ISBN 978-1-934941-17-1
  1. Snakes as pets. 2. Poisonous snakes. I. Title.
  SF459.S5F57 2008
  639.3'96--dc22

                                                2008013586

Red and Black Publishers, PO Box 7542, St Petersburg, Florida, 33734

Contact us at: info@RedandBlackPublishers.com

Printed and manufactured in the United States of America

All photos by author.

Contents

Introduction

When I first told a few friends and family members that I was working on a booklet demonstrating the proper techniques for keeping venomous snakes, the reaction was immediate, unanimous and predictable: "Omigod!! Some kid is gonna read it and get himself killed!!!!!" "Isn't it dangerous to put information like that out to the public???" "You're gonna get sued!!!"

So why write about keeping venomous snakes? My primary reason, ironically, is to *discourage* inexperienced people from trying it. Over the past ten years, the hobby of herpetoculture has grown exponentially. Predictably, as the interest in snakes and other reptiles has grown, so too has the interest in venomous snakes (known to afficionados as "hot" snakes). As a reptile writer, I get several requests every month from people who want to know about keeping rattlesnakes or cobras or whatever. Virtually every local herpetological society in the United States has its contingent of "fang freaks". A surprising number of venomous species are being captive bred by amateur enthusiasts, and a number of venomous breeders and dealers can be found on the Internet and through ads in the reptile hobby magazines. Venomous snakes are also readily obtainable at local herp swaps and shows, as well as at the national reptile expo held in eastern Pennsylvania twice each year.

Venomous snakes, like this Timber Rattlesnake, are more widely available to amateur keepers than you might think.

This increase in the availability of venomous snakes has unfortunately not been matched by a corresponding increase in the availability of good practical information about keeping them. Many of these serpents are being purchased by inexperienced people who have no real idea what they are getting into, and no real idea how to go about the business of keeping a potentially dangerous or lethal snake. The primary purpose of this booklet is to give that information, to let every potential hot keeper know, up front, exactly what he or she is getting into. Again and again, I will emphasize that keeping hot snakes is serious business, not to be entered into lightly. Your first mistake may very well be your last.

I pull no punches here. This is not a game. These snakes can kill. While every keeper has his or her own individual way of doing things, I will be blunt here about what works for me and what doesn't, and why. I'll also be blunt about the consequences of a mistake. This is not done for the purposes of sensationalism; it is done to show everyone, clearly and coldly, what happens if you flub up. If you make a mistake with a venomous snake, there is no second chance.

Although many herpers develop an interest in hots, and many of these may decide that they might want to give it a try, I have found that most prospective hot keepers lose interest once they learn how much equipment, money and knowledge is actually necessary, and once they really deeply understand what the real-world consequences of a single mistake could be.

In effect, if you are thinking about keeping venomous snakes, the goal of this booklet is to try and talk you out of it.

If, however, despite my efforts to talk you out of it, you do join the ranks of the "fang freaks", I hope that the information here will serve as a useful supplement, as your "snake mentor" shows you the ropes and gives you live hands-on experience under a watchful eye.

Most of the methods depicted here are not flashy (and I strongly discourage anyone from trying the ones that are). You will not look like "The Crocodile Hunter" as he casually carries lethal snakes around by the tail. By nature, I am a very cautious and conservative snake keeper. I do not mess with snakes I am not comfortable with, and I do not give the snakes I *do* mess with the opportunity to poke any holes anywhere in me. I suppose that is why I am still alive, and still have all my fingers and toes. Some of my snake-keeping acquaintances do not.

Things to Keep in Mind

First things first. Here are some things that every potential hot keeper must consider *before* he or she gets that first snake.

(1) Why do you want to keep a venomous snake? For use in educational shows or talks? Captive breeding for conservation? Or because it shows the world what a macho kind of guy you are? If you want to keep a hot snake because it's "cool" or to impress people, then you are not ready to keep them at all. Go take karate lessons instead.

(2) Where are you going to get your hot snake? Catch it yourself? In many areas that's illegal. It can also kill you if you don't

know what you are doing. And if you need to ask where you can buy a venomous snake, then you're not ready to be keeping one.

(3) How much snake experience do you have? Keeping a venomous snake is not the same as keeping a corn snake or ball python or even a burmese python. Can you work with a really nasty snake like a water snake or coachwhip, regularly, routinely, and reliably without getting bitten? If you can't go at least a year without being bitten by a coachwhip, racer or something similar, you're not ready to be handling hot snakes.

If you are keeping a venomous snake, like this Eastern Diamondback Rattlesnake, be sure you are doing it for the right reasons.

(4) Is it legal to keep a venomous snake where you live? Many localities have laws against dangerous animals in general or venomous snakes in particular. Usually these are passed after some bonehead gets bitten by his pet puff adder or something. Don't even *try* to keep a hot snake where it isn't legal to do so. When anything happens, having your snake confiscated and destroyed is about the *best* you can hope for. You might just find your butt in the slammer. And in any case the reptile hobby doesn't need the bad publicity that will result from your stupid actions.

(5) Can you properly house a venomous snake? A single-piece sliding door cage, designed to be escape-proof, is an absolute necessity

for keeping any venomous snake, and they are not cheap. That aquarium with a screen lid on top, weighted down with a couple of bricks, won't cut it. In addition, your "hot room" will need to be modified to make it absolutely 100% escape-proof, and that can require some modifications to the door, windows and baseboards. Can't afford secure housing? Then you can't afford the snake.

(6) Do you live in a place where others can be potentially exposed to the snake? Perhaps *you* think you know enough to handle a hot snake without being bitten, and perhaps *you* are willing to risk death/disfigurement—but what about your spouse, your kids, or your neighbors? When your snake bites anybody around you, you can expect some very nasty legal actions that will occupy you for a good chunk of your life. Better have lots of liability insurance, and keep it paid up.

Every venomous snake keeper should expect to be bitten at some point in time, and plan accordingly.

(7) Who is your "mentor"? Which experienced hot snake keeper is available for you to learn firsthand, under a watchful eye, how to use a snake stick, how to use a catchbox, how to do such routine tasks as feeding and cleaning? If you think you are going to learn this "on your own", forget it. You'll be nothing but a danger to yourself and others.

(8) What are your plans for handling the snake when it comes time for things like changing the water and feeding? Who can you trust to be your partner, to be there every time you open the snake cage? Who will, in the event of an accident, have the necessary experience to handle and confine the snake so it doesn't escape? Planning on doing this yourself? What happens when you collapse on the floor instead?

(9) What about when you get bitten? Does the hospital have a ready supply of antivenom for the species you want to keep? Don't even *think* about depending on the local zoo for your supply—they need it themselves, and they don't appreciate having some bozo taking their entire supply of antivenom to save his sorry butt (meanwhile leaving the zoo staff without any antivenom in case *they* have an accident).

(10) How's your bank account? Antivenom alone runs several hundred dollars per vial, and a really serious bite can require as many as twenty or twenty five vials. Plus you'll have to pay the good doctor, the lab bills, the cost of a hospital bed, etc etc etc. You should plan on leaving at least $15,000 in the bank at all times. When you get seriously bitten, you'll need it.

(11) What if the snake gets sick? Do you have an experienced veterinarian near you that will be willing to treat your snake if it gets an infection, or if it retains an eyecap, or has an incomplete shed?

Let me be blunt. Venomous snakes kill people. There is nothing theoretical about that. If you are deluding yourself into thinking "I'll never get bit", think again. It will happen. Count on it.

Being dead lasts for a long time. Don't be stupid. If you can't deal seriously and thoroughly with every one of the concerns listed above, then you're not ready to keep a venomous snake.

Devenomed Snakes

In many areas, "devenomed" or "venomoid" snakes are available. These are hot snakes that have been surgically altered by a veterinarian, either through a "tubal ligation", in which the duct leading from the venom gland to the fang is severed, or through complete removal of the venom gland using a laser. This has the effect of rendering that particular snake unable to inject any venom.

There are health risks associated with the operation. Even the tiniest cut during the surgery can lead to infection which is difficult to treat and often fatal. Stress-prone snakes do not handle the operation very well. There is some question about whether removal of the venom can lead to impairment of digestion, since venom does play a role in "pre-digesting" prey. Another complication is that removing the venom also removes the snake's method of killing its prey, so it will have to be fed pre-killed food from now on—and many snakes refuse to eat pre-killed prey. In my experience, it seems that the elapids (cobras) tolerate the operation much more successfully than viperids do. The more responsible veterinarians will only perform the surgery on long-term captives that are already feeding well on pre-killed food.

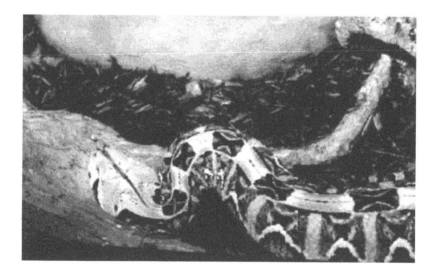

The Gaboon Viper is a popular venomous species that is available as a "devenomed" snake.

De-venomed snakes still possess fangs (like all of the snake's teeth, the fangs are periodically shed and replaced), and a bite from a large devenomed viperid is still a painful affair. There have also been documented instances where devenomed snakes have re-gained their ability to inject venom, either because they had a second duct that the surgeon missed, or because a portion of the venom gland was inadvertently left behind and regenerated. Venomoids should be checked every few months to insure that they are still unable to inject venom. I make it a strict habit to treat all devenomed snakes as if they were still hot.

Venomoid snakes are extremely controversial among hot keepers. Many fang freaks view de-venomed snakes as a sacrilege, and argue that these animals should not be mutilated in this way, and that de-venomed snakes encourage ownership of these animals by unprepared and irresponsible people. My own view is that no venomous snake should be surgically altered just to make a "pet" out of it. The only de-venomed snakes I keep are used for educational talks and shows, where their lack of venom serves as a safety precaution (and also makes my insurance company a lot happier).

For beginning hot keepers, learning the tricks of the trade on a devenomed snake gives a valuable added level of safety (particularly if you are dealing with difficult snakes like elapids), allowing you to make all your mistakes with a snake that can't kill you. However, it should be noted that many of the challenges in handling a hot snake are mental, and, psychologically, you will not act the same around a devenomed snake if you know it cannot hurt you. Learning basic handling techniques on a venomoid snake is fine, but if you really want to learn how to handle hot snakes, there's no substitute for the real thing.

Basic Safety Rules

Here is where we list all the general rules that *must* be followed whenever you are near a hot snake of any sort. Although most of these are simple common sense, I know personally hot snake keepers who have, at one time or another, violated nearly every one of these. Some have paid an awful high price for their momentary lapse of reason.

The number one rule, the Golden Rule, the Prime Directive, is simple, basic and obvious—*never allow any part of your body to get within the strike range of a hot snake.* Ever.

Rule number two—never handle a venomous snake alone. If you have an accident, you'll need an experienced person with you to help confine the snake, to render first aid, and to help get you to a hospital.

Rule number three—never open a snake's cage if you are anything less than 100% mentally and physically "sharp". Do not under any circumstances attempt to handle a hot snake if you have had a few beers (a large proportion of bites from venomous snakes involve alcohol), if you've been smoking some weed, if you're tired, if you had a fight with your girlfriend, if you're in a hurry to get to a movie, if you're distracted by an upcoming final exam, if . . . you get the idea. When you are exposing yourself to a venomous animal, you will need all of your wits about you, and *anything* that impairs your judgment or slows your reflexes is a potential danger to you.

Although the Brown Tree Snake is not lethally dangerous, it must still be treated with respect and caution.

The final safety rule—know your limits. Choose a species that is appropriate to your level of experience and ability. If you are an inexperienced keeper, limit yourself to those species that don't present an unacceptable level of challenge for you. If you attempt to keep a taipan or Egyptian cobra as your first snake, you are operating way outside your limits. Also, know your physical limits. If you are a person of small stature, you will find wrestling with an eight foot Eastern diamondback to be somewhat difficult. Me, I'm 47 years old and my reflexes aren't what they used to be, so I stay away from snakes like cobras that demand quick reactions. I've taken a lot of good-natured ribbing from snake-keeping friends about that, but this simple precaution has kept me healthy, happy and out of trouble so far.

Difficult species such as this Monocled Cobra should not be kept by inexperienced or inadequately-trained people.

Realize what you are capable of, and what you are *not* capable of. Don't rush things. Stay comfortably within your limits, and gain experience before you move on to more challenging things.

Housing

When it comes to housing a venomous snake, there are three primary considerations that absolutely must be kept uppermost in mind. They are (1) security, (2) security and (3) security. If you are keeping hot snakes, you are 100% responsible not only for your own safety, but also that of everyone else who happens to be in the vicinity. Your snakes cannot present even a hint of danger to yourself, your housemates, your visitors, or your neighbors. Anything less than perfect escape-proof confinement is unforgivable, and any negligence or oversight on your part that allows a dangerous snake to escape from your control is criminal—both legally and morally. I personally am a security fanatic, and place the safety of my neighbors and friends above my own. For that reason, my snake room is sealed so tightly that even a housefly would have a hard time getting out of there, and the cages I use are, I believe, the very best available. If I get tagged in my snake room, even if I drop dead on the spot, that snake will not be able to leave that room to present a threat to anyone else.

Safety and security are not areas that you want to cut corners on. You are risking your life (and the lives of those around you) on the dependability of these safety and confinement measures. Nothing less than perfection will do.

Security begins even before you obtain any snakes. You will need a "hot room", which is an escape-proof area where all of your venomous snakes will be housed. Ideally, this should be a small shedlike building that is not attached to the main house. In practice, a spare bedroom or utility room can often be modified sufficiently to serve as a hot room. The larger your snake room is, the better---you want a lot of open floor space where you can maneuver without bumping into a lot of clutter. Your hot room should contain your snakes, your snake-keeping equipment, and nothing else.

The first task in "snakeproofing" a room is to seal off any hole, duct or vent, no matter how small. This includes things like heating grills, air conditioner vents and the edges of doors and windows. Snakes can squeeze themselves through some remarkably small gaps, so your hot room must be sealed tightly to prevent any possibility of escape. In considering potential escape avenues, you must assume that your snake will be able to levitate itself to surprising heights (even up sheer walls), that it is strong enough to push its way through all but the toughest barriers, and that if there is *any* potential avenue of escape, no matter how slight, the snake will head unerringly straight for it.

The most secure snake rooms are windowless. Since most keepers convert a spare bedroom as their hot room, however, there will usually be at least one window to deal with. All of the windows must be completely covered with wire screen (I prefer to use two layers of screen---a layer of quarter-inch mesh hardware cloth over top a layer of ordinary mosquito-mesh window screen, a combination which gives both strength and impenetrability). The edges of these screens must be tightly sealed to the window frame with slats of wood, to prevent even the smallest of snakes from squeezing under the screen and wriggling through. Screen on the inside of the window makes it more difficult for snakes to push the screen edges outwards to escape. For extra security, you can seal off both the inside and outside of the window frame (note that this will prevent you from opening and closing the window). Any openings in the walls or floors, such as air conditioning or heating vents, get the same treatment.

It is absolutely necessary that there be no holes or openings of any sort into the space between the walls, since having a hot snake

---

inside the building structure, free to move unseen from room to room, is an exceedingly dangerous situation. Any such holes must be repaired to make them as strong as the rest of the wall.

Another often-overlooked avenue of possible escape is the small gap often found around plumbing pipes or electrical conduits. These must be completely sealed with caulk. It is also a good idea to caulk around the screen frames covering the windows and vents.

The floor of your hot room should be vinyl plastic sheet, linoleum tile or hardwood. Carpeting should be avoided, as it is then possible for a snake to squeeze under the edge and be lost under the carpet. Any gaps between the floor edge and the walls must be securely caulked.

The door to the hot room is another area where your security concerns should be heavily focused. The door must fit tightly into its frame, with no gaps anywhere around the perimeter. If you can see light shining between the door and its frame, it needs to be tighter. The bottom of the door should receive special attention, since there is often a gap between the door and the floor. Seal this off with a strip of hardwood nailed to the floor so the door just barely clears it. For extra security, install hard rubber "weather stripping" on the door.

For maximum safety, the door should ideally have a window that allows all of the cages to be viewed from outside, allowing you to determine in advance if there have been any escapes. The light switch should be located just outside the room, avoiding the necessity of opening the door and momentarily fumbling for the switch. Do not place the light switch on the other side of the room—if you need to cross the floor in the dark to turn on the light, you might be in for a very unpleasant surprise if you have an escape. Keeping your snake-handling equipment on a rack next to the light switch allows it to be always within easy reach.

Needless to say, the door to your hot room should be securely locked (deadbolted) whenever you are not in it, and you should have the only keys. Hide a spare set somewhere in the house. Do not allow anybody to have unauthorized access to your hot room. Place a prominent warning sign on the door, something like "DANGER!! This room contains venomous animals." If your snake room is at ground level, you would not be paranoid to have a good alarm system rigged up to the windows to prevent anyone from breaking in. Some further precautions—install a phone in the room, with the phone number of the nearest hospital emergency room (and directions to same) taped next to it. A spare set of car keys hanging here will save precious minutes when you need to get to a hospital NOW.

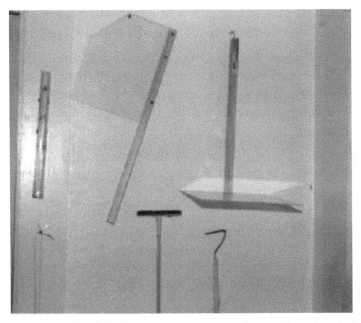

Hanging your snake-handling equipment on the wall makes it instantly available when you need it.

Now that we have the hot room all set up and tightly secured, we will need some cages. On the matter of cages for venomous snakes, there are almost as many opinions about what is suitable as there are hot snake keepers to argue about it. This booklet I give my opinion, which other hot keepers may or may not agree with. But there is one point that all hot keepers will concede—a properly designed and secured cage is the first, best and most important line of defense against escapes and accidents. No corner-cutting here either. You will be betting your life on the security of your snake cage. Only the very best will do.

I have seen a variety of different cages used by venomous snake keepers, everything from simple Rubbermaid sweater boxes with some air holes drilled in the side (suitable for only youngsters of the most docile species) to huge elaborate hand-made wooden enclosures with locking sliding glass doors (suitable for large and fast arboreal snakes like mambas and boomslangs). Since I don't keep these large arboreal elapids, I won't speak to that, and will leave discussion of such cages to those who are more adept with a hammer and saw (and either more brave or more foolhardy) than I am. The species I keep consist almost entirely of small-to-midsize terrestrial snakes (mostly pit vipers) and small arboreal viperids, and in my view, there is only one suitable choice for caging these reptiles. The Neodesha cages, which were designed specifically for keeping venomous snakes, consist of one piece of molded plastic with a lockable sliding glass door. They are, in my view, the very best cages available. The Neodesha arboreal cages, with triple latches on a lockable glass door, are perfectly suited for arboreal vipers. Others may disagree with me, but for my part, nothing but Neodesha cages ever enter my hot snake room.

Neodesha has, unfortunately, gone out of business, but pre-owned cages can still be found. One good place to look would be the classified ads at websites like www.kingsnake.com, or at online sales areas like eBay.

Neodesha cages are specifically designed for keeping venomous snakes

If you can't find a pre-owned Neodesha cage anywhere, a possible substitute might be the molded plastic cages made by Vision Herpetological. These are available in a wide variety of sizes, and have their own custom-made rack systems. I've not used any of these cages myself, but the snakers I've talked with who do use them point out that the overlap in the middle where the double doors meet is a potential security concern if you are keeping small or thin-bodied snakes.

The Neodesha cages have several characteristics which I like. The one-piece sliding glass door offers terrific security, while at the same time the slanted front allows a good view of the cage contents, even if the cage is on a lower shelf. It comes with provisions for padlocking the cage. The rounded corners and plastic one-piece construction allow for easy cleaning. The screen mesh at the top is large enough to provide decent ventilation (and allows the keeper to pour water into a bowl or to use a sprayer to mist the inside of the cage without having to open it—a great security advantage), yet is not so large that it presents an unacceptable danger of a viper striking at you through the screen. One disadvantage to the Neodesha cages, though, is that they cannot be stacked atop each other and therefore require a set of shelves. Another disadvantage (shared by all front-opening cages) is that they allow fast snakes like cobras to explode out the front of the cage, at floor level, as soon as you open it. (However, since I recommend using catchboxes on all of the fast elapids anyway, this doesn't present an insurmountable problem for me). Neodesha cages are also a bit pricey (but are in my mind worth every nickel).

Some further security precautions. All of the individual cages should be securely padlocked, and kept locked any time you are not actually servicing the cage, even if the door to the snake room is kept locked. Each cage should also be clearly labeled with the number and name (both common name and Latin name) of the snake(s) they contain. (Incidentally, unless you are attempting to breed the snakes, it is my recommendation that each cage should contain only one snake, to limit the number of potential moving targets you need to track whenever you open the cage—especially important with fast-moving snakes like cobras or other elapids.)

If you keep your cages on a rack, it is a good idea to always leave the bottom space empty, so any snakes that get away from you will not be able to zip off and hide behind a rack of cages. If you have any large heavy cages that sit directly on the floor, they should be located right up against the wall, and the space between the cage and the wall should be securely sealed with caulk or wood stripping to prevent any snakes from wedging themselves behind the cage.

Housing a venomous snake is the one area where you absolutely cannot make any mistakes.

Handling

For most herpers, the word "handling" implies freehandling a snake with bare hands. This is emphatically *not* applicable to any venomous snake. We've all seen films and photos of snake keepers walking around with the head of an angry rattler or cobra pinned in his fingers, or carrying cobras (or worse) around by the tail. Let me be clear about this: any nonprofessional (and most professionals) who even attempts to casually freehandle any sort of venomous snake in this manner has rocks in his head. You should plan on going your entire life without ever touching any of your venomous snakes. Ever. Not even once.

There are of course occasions when you will have no choice but to physically contact the snake, usually for reasons of health care. Far from being a pleasant interaction, such occasions are nerve-wracking, dreaded and incredibly dangerous. A huge proportion of bites result from mistakes made while keepers are attempting to hold a snake with bare hands. Unless you are "milking" the snake for research purposes or unless you must treat the snake for a medical condition and have no safer alternative, there is absolutely no reason why you should ever need to touch a venomous snake in any way, shape or form. In fact, you should never even allow any part of your body to come within the strike range of any venomous snake. That's what handling equipment is for.

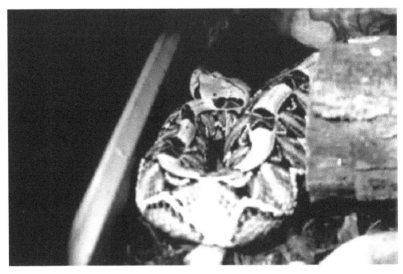

Never attempt to handle a dangerous snake like this Gaboon Viper until you have sufficient training and experience.

Now I will let you in on a little secret: the best venomous snake keepers — the ones who live the longest and have the fewest scars – don't handle their snakes at all if they can help it. Not even on a stick or with tongs. Why not? To begin with, it's not very healthful for the snake. Snakes can become very stressed by handling, and find the whole process to be horribly frightening. Handling is particularly risky for finicky eaters like coral snakes and some of the copperheads, or for delicate snakes like some of the tree vipers. Getting these guys to eat regularly is enough of a challenge, without having the poor little thing barf up its last meal every time you hook him out of his cage.

As we have seen, a well-designed cage allows such routine tasks as watering and misting to be done without the need to remove the snake or even open the cage. This greatly reduces the number of times it becomes necessary to move or handle the reptile. For those occasions when the snake simply must be removed for some reason, there are alternative methods of confining and moving it that are less stressful and do not leave it feeling exposed, vulnerable, and apt to strike.

Needless to say, being able to work in the cage without the potential risks of moving the snake on a hook is far more healthful for the snake keeper, as well.

Since I use my snakes for educational talks and shows, where they must be displayed in the open, my snakes get a lot more "stick time" than most. For most keepers, though, there are not very many good reasons why a venomous snake should ever have to be handled on a hook. There are safer and less stressful alternatives.

Here, then, are the most common methods of moving a venomous snake from one point to another.

Snake hooks

The snakestick is the standard piece of equipment for handling venomous snakes.

The time-honored traditional way of handling venomous snakes and still, under some circumstances, one of the easiest. A snake hook, also known as a snakestick, is a long thin piece of metal with a curved hook at one end, used to lift and handle venomous snakes. Snakesticks are one of the few venomous snake-keeping items that are readily available commercially, since nonvenomous snake keepers also use them for aggressive or nippy species. A number of different lengths are available, from small sizes for juvenile snakes to big two-handed ones for handling heavy pythons or boas (these huge sticks being too heavy and cumbersome for use with venomous snakes). Most commercial snakesticks are made from one piece of tempered steel, with a rubber handle that resembles a golf club. A few models have sections that screw together and can be collapsed or extended for varying lengths.

At minimum, you will want a stick that is a foot or so longer than the longest strike range of the snake(s) you will be handling (generally about half the body length, but this can vary widely from species to species—some species being able to strike virtually their entire body length). For extra safety, try to always use a stick that is at least as long as the snake itself. Snakesticks longer than 3-4 ft, though, are heavy and difficult to maneuver, so if your snake is longer than this, you will need to use two sticks at the same time to control it, or one stick coupled with "tailing".

Some very workable snakesticks can be made at home (get used to this; most of the equipment you will need for venomous snakes is not available commercially—after all, it's not like there's much of a demand for it—and you will probably end up making most of your equipment yourself). I have a set of sticks in varying lengths that I made from 3/8 inch and ¼ inch steel welding rod that I bent into shape. They cost me less than two bucks each and have served me well.

To make a snakestick from a metal bar, bend the last 4-6 inches (depending on the size of the snake you will be handling and how you will be handling it—"tailing" a snake requires a somewhat wider hook) to the side, leaving a deep wide U-shape at about a 45-degree angle to the straight shaft. Then bend the shaft back so that it is perpendicular to the short straight section of the hook. The line made by the shaft should intercept the straight section of the hook at about the midpoint. Hammer or grind the very tip of the hook so it is rounded and flattened, making it easier to slide underneath the snake's body without injuring it on any sharp edges or points. Finish it up by wrapping some cloth tape or a leather band around the handle to improve the grip. The snakesticks I use most often, to handle viperid snakes in the 1.5 to 3 ft range, have four-inch hooks and measure about 30 inches long overall. They are made from 36-inch sections of 3/8 inch steel rod. Standard-sized snakesticks are about 40 inches long and can be made from 48-inch sections of steel rod.

For handling very small snakes or young juveniles less than a foot long, a workable snake hook can be made from a wire coathanger. Cut a 6-8 inch section of straight wire from the coathanger and bend it into an appropriate hook about three inches wide. Attach this securely to a straight wooden dowel about 1.5 feet long and a quarter-inch in diameter. The shaft of the hook can be hammered into the end of the dowel like a nail to hold it, or the shaft of the hook can be laid alongside the dowel and wrapped with wire to bind it tightly. Be absolutely certain that the hook is securely attached—you do not want it to be able to rotate or turn inside the shaft when the weight of a snake is on the hook.

Handling a Dusky Pygmy Rattlesnake with a snakestick.

Using a snakestick effectively, particularly on fast or agile snakes, is more an art form than a science, and is a skill that cannot be learned by reading a book or website, but only by lots of practice. Beginners should start off by using their snakestick on nonvenomous snakes, to get accustomed to the feel of it. Small ball pythons make good practice subjects, as they are roughly the body shape and weight of most vipers and rattlesnakes. If you practice using a snake hook on a fast nonvenomous colubrid such as a racer or coachwhip, you'll quickly learn why stick-handling an agile venomous snake, like a cobra or mamba, is a very dangerous business.

To handle a snake using a stick, slide the tip of the hook under the body, about halfway down, and gently but firmly lift the snake off the ground. If you do this too slowly, the snake will glide off as you lift it. Since most vipers and rattlesnakes are terrestrial, being lifted off the ground triggers an instinctive fear of falling, and they will grip the hook tightly with their bodies to hang on. This is what you want. As long as you keep the snake high enough off the ground that he doesn't think he can get down, he will most often hang there motionless (perhaps striking in your direction once in a while) while you move him to a holding bin or bag. As you move the snake, remember that it is still capable of striking, and that anything within the sphere of the snake's "strike radius" is in danger. Watch your feet, your shoulders, your face, and your other arm. Also watch any other people in the vicinity.

Once you've lowered the snake into the enclosure, slide the hook out from under him. Done.

In general, the various pit vipers are not terribly difficult to handle, and often don't have any problem staying "on stick". Some individual snakes, however, may try to scramble down from the hook, or may try to scamper off while you are lifting them from the floor. A few species may even move directly towards you with the full intention of attacking. Such snakes are known as "runners", and nobody likes handling them. The cobras and other elapids are particularly apt to be "runny". Sometimes, runners can be controlled using two sticks, allowing the snake to glide from one to the other as it is being carried. If the snake is too active for even this, then you will have to "tail" him if you want to use a hook on him. Also, if the snake is so long that you are still within his strike range while holding the stick, you will need two sticks, or you will need to tail him.

Some snakes, particularly the arboreal ones, may try to climb up the shaft of the snakestick towards you. You will find a second snakestick handy to prevent that from happening. Finally, heavy-bodied snakes such as gaboon vipers, puff adders, cottonmouths and some of the rattlers, can be injured by the weight of their bodies pressing down on a hook. Using two hooks on these snakes allows the weight to be distributed, lessening the chances of injury.

We've all seen films of people using their snake hooks to pin a rattler behind the head before reaching down to pick it up. This is a major no-no. Done improperly, this can cause severe injury to the snake's spine and nerves. Done improperly, the snake can also cause severe injury to *you*. It should be emphasized here that pinning a snake is an *extremely* hazardous procedure that should not be done unless it is absolutely necessary. If you must pin a snake (usually for medical reasons), use a purpose-built pinning stick (described later) to do it.

L-Hooks

Once you begin to hook arboreal vipers with your snake stick, you will quickly learn that getting them on the stick is the easy part—it is getting them *off* again that becomes tricky. Quite often, the little nipper will wrap his tail tightly around the hook and refuse to let go, no matter what prodding and poking you do. To solve this problem, many hot keepers keep a set of modified snake hooks for use specifically with arboreal vipers. These consist of hooks with a straight 90-degree bend, like the letter "L", instead of the curved hook found on standard snake sticks. Without the curved part to hang onto, most arboreals can be gently nudged with a second stick and slid right off the straight hook into a bag or their cage.

Because the L-sticks don't have the deep U-shaped "throat" that the standard snakesticks have, there is nothing to support the weight of the snake. If you make the mistake of lifting the end of the stick too high, therefore, you will face the possible hazard that the snake will unwillingly slide down the shaft, directly towards you. Not a good thing. Be careful when handling a snake on an L-hook to always keep the end of the stick lower than your hand.

L-sticks work best when used in pairs, with one stick used to pick the snake off the other.

Tailing

As noted above, many of the elapids such as cobras do not deal with snakesticks very well, and will often refuse to stay "on stick", even if you try to use two sticks on them. Another potential problem comes from the large heavy-bodied vipers, which can be injured by the sheer bulk of their body weight pressing the hook of a snakestick into their ribs. In that case, many snake keepers resort to a practice known as "tailing". Let me be clear at the outset—tailing a venomous snake is *very* dangerous and puts you at a significantly increased risk of being bitten. Don't try this at home without lots of practice and training under the eye of an experienced mentor.

Tailing a cobra or krait takes advantage of a peculiar quirk of elapid anatomy. Because of the structure of their spine and musculature, elapids strike by rearing the front parts of their bodies off the ground and then falling forward. This means that as long as your body is outside this "danger arc", the snake cannot reach you. It also means that elapids cannot strike upwards. If, therefore, you grasp a small or medium-sized cobra by the tail and lift it straight up off the ground, it will not be able to easily reach up and bite the hand that is holding it. This is known as "tailing".

The snake will still be able to rear up the front part of its body and strike outwards, though, so you will need to be careful to hold it away from your body so it cannot reach you. If the snake is very long, you may not be able to hold it far enough away to be out of its strike radius. And in any case, if held for too long a time, the snake will be able to climb partway up its own body, or swing itself wildly until your hand or body is within reach. To prevent all this from happening, use a snakestick or tongs to hold the head and front half of the snake's body at a safe distance from you. If you grasp the tail and keep its body taut between your hand and the hook, the snake will not be able to run off the stick and will not be able to reach back and get you. It often helps to jiggle the snake around a little bit while you are carrying it, which keeps it off balance and prevents it from attempting to climb off (or up) the stick.

As we have seen, large heavy-bodied viperids like gaboons, puff adders, cottonmouths and some of the rattlers cannot easily be handled using a snakestick. It is possible to tail these as well, but this is *extremely* hazardous, since the viperids are fully capable of reaching up and biting the hand that is holding them. You will need a snake hook or tongs to hold the front part of the body safely away from you and keep it there. The hand holding the tail supports most of the snake's weight, while the hook is used to control the "sharp end" of the snake. Large viperids are incredibly strong, and you will get quite a workout trying to tail one. Don't underestimate their strength or overestimate yours. If you lose your grip on the tail or if the hook fails to control the front end, you will be faced with an angered snake in close proximity to you. Not very healthful.

Tailing a large viperid, like this Florida Cottonmouth, is a hazardous and extremely risky task.

Tailing looks easy, and properly done it is much safer than attempting to control a large elapid with only a snake hook. Nevertheless, it is risky and should only be done if no safer method can be used. It is far safer to confine and move elapids and large viperids with a catchbox.

Grabsticks

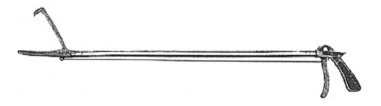

Grabsticks or snake tongs are commercially available.

The grabstick, also known as the snake tongs, is a mechanical device with a pair of jaws that can be closed around the snake's body to hold it. For some reason, inexperienced keepers tend to like these, and view them as if they were the safest method for moving a venomous snake around. They are also the preferred tool of the professional "rattlesnake catchers" who gather snakes for "roundups" (often illegally by dousing the snake's den with gasoline and extracting it as it tries to escape).

Grabsticks are often used by rattlesnake collectors, but they can cause severe injury to the snake.

Since it may be difficult to control the amount of pressure in the jaws, it is easy to break ribs or otherwise severely injure snakes with these things. (If you look closely at the rattlers in a "roundup", you will see that nearly all of them have skin tears and injuries on their body where they were grasped by a pair of snake tongs.) Most snakes react violently to being firmly gripped by a grabstick, as opposed to simply being "guided" by a snake hook, and will thrash around a lot, which only increases the chances of internal injury.

If you must use tongs, gluing some foam rubber padding onto the inside of the tong jaws will help prevent injuries. Take care to always grasp the snake near mid-body. Grabbing the snake behind the head and lifting it off the ground may cause its body weight or thrashing to pull the skull away from the ball-and-socket joint that connects it to the spine, resulting in instant death.

I don't like tongs and don't use them. As a last resort, they may provide a safer (for you) alternative to tailing a large or aggressive serpent. But there are safer and less injury-prone ways to move a snake.

Pinning Stick

The pinning stick

When most people think of "handling" a venomous snake, they picture a lab-coated technician using a snakestick to pin the back of a snake's neck to the floor before picking it up, hooking its fangs over a glass vial, and squeezing out the venom. Although handling a snake like this is necessary for production of antivenom in a lab, there are only the rarest of occasions when a venomous snake keeper will need to restrain a snake in this manner (one reason would be for medical treatment of mouth rot or retained eyecaps, or to force-feed a snake), and even then, there are usually alternative methods available that are safer for both you and the snake. Pinning and restraining a hot snake's head in your fingers is an excellent way to get bitten.

If it becomes necessary to pin a snake, this should be done with a special-purpose pinning stick, rather than an ordinary snakestick or L-stick. Metal snake hooks can cause a tremendous amount of damage to the snake if they are used improperly. A purpose-built pinning stick takes the form of a T with a long handle (mine is 36 inches long) and a short crossbar at the end, about five inches long and half an inch wide. The bottom of the crossbar is padded with foam rubber.

Using the pinning stick to restrain a Dusky Pygmy Rattlesnake.

Another type of pinning stick has a short "Y" shaped end, with a tube of surgical rubber strung across the gap. The tension in the rubber is adjusted by tightening or loosening the tube. These are less prone to cause injury than are the solid pinning sticks, but also take a bit of practice to get the tension and pressure just right.

To use the pinning stick properly, you will need to hook the snake onto a soft area like a carpet, a folded towel, or a pad of foam rubber.

Carefully press the crossbar of the pinning stick across the back of the snake's head, just behind the eyes, and press down hard enough that the snake cannot pull its head out from underneath, but not so hard that you injure the snake.

Once the snake is securely pinned, you will need to reach down and restrain it with your fingers.

The proper grip for holding a viperid snake.

There are two different grips for restraining a venomous snake. The "two finger" grip consists of placing your thumb on the top of the pinned snake's head and encircling its throat with your index finger. Squeezing your fingers together clamps the snake between your thumb and forefinger, preventing it from turning and biting you. You may have to use your other hand to control the snake's body to prevent it from thrashing around and either injuring itself or gaining enough leverage to pull its head out of your grip. This grip should only be used on short-fanged snakes like elapids. If used on a viperid, the longer fangs will be able to reach your forefinger and get you.

For vipers, you will need to use the "three finger" grip. Once the snake is pinned, place your index finger on top of its head and place your thumb and middle finger on either side, just behind the jaws. Your remaining fingers will curl around the snake's neck. Use your other hand to control the snake's body and prevent it from thrashing around.

Pinning is a hazardous operation, and a high proportion of the snakebites suffered by hot keepers are the result of accidents and mistakes made while pinning and restraining (usually unnecessarily) a snake. Agile snakes like cobras will twist and thrash violently. Just getting a pinning stick on them properly will be quite a task, and if they succeed in loosening your grip while you are holding them, you are in serious trouble. Large vipers like rattlers and Gaboons are very strong and powerful animals, and if it comes to a flat-out wrestling match with one of these, you will lose. The riskiest part of the procedure comes after you have grasped the snake in your fingers, but before you remove the pinning stick. If your grip isn't good, you will be in close proximity to the fangs of a thoroughly enraged snake. Cobras can cause difficulty in pinning because they will be "hooding" as you are trying to get a good grip on their neck. A large number of bites result from grasping the snake too far back on the neck, giving it enough room to turn its head and tag you, or getting your fingers too close to the front of a viper's head, allowing it to poke a fang out the side of its mouth and into your finger. Make sure you pin the snake properly right behind the eyes, make sure you are grasping the snake just behind the angle of the jaws, and make sure your grip is secure before removing the pinning stick.

Once you have the snake securely gripped, your risks are not yet over—you will need at some point to put the snake down. The safest way to do this is the opposite of what you did to pin it. Lay the snake's body down on the floor, hold the snake's head still, lay your pinning stick across the back of its head, take your fingers away, then lift the stick away. The more swiftly and smoothly you can do this, the less the snake will thrash around and the less chances of it (or you) being injured. It is almost a given that the snake will attempt a defensive strike at you as soon as it is freed. Be prepared and be out of range. And watch your feet.

Another method, more risky but used by some keepers, is to place the snake's body in its enclosure and then simply "toss" the snake's head away and (quickly) pulling your hands out of harm's way. I know at least one keeper, though, who was bitten in this manner when he wasn't quite fast enough and the snake turned and bit him in mid-air as it fell.

My advice? Don't ever pin any snake unless there is absolutely positively no other alternative to save the life of the snake.

Tubes

These handy little devices are essential when it becomes necessary to treat a venomous snake for a number of medical problems, including ticks, retained sheds, or injections. Tubes are far less stressful for the snake than pinning and restraining (and far less dangerous for the keeper).

Snake tubes consist of a clear acrylic or plastic tube, about half as long and just barely wider than the snake's body. Along its length, the snake tube should have a number of holes drilled, varying in diameter from 1/8 to 3/8 inch. One end of the tube is securely sealed. Many keepers like to secure a snake tube to a tabletop, which allows them to hold the snake's body with one hand and leaving the other hand free. Others prefer having an assistant to securely hold the tube and snake while the work is being done.

In theory, the idea of a snake tube is simple. The snake's head enters the open end of the tube. Once the snake's body is all the way inside the tube, grasp both tube and snake securely, preventing the snake from backing out. Since the snake doesn't have room inside the tube to turn its head around, it is securely trapped, and the holes in the side of the tube give you access for giving shots, picking off ticks, etc. When you are done with your task, place the snake's body back in its cage, pull off the tube, and voila.

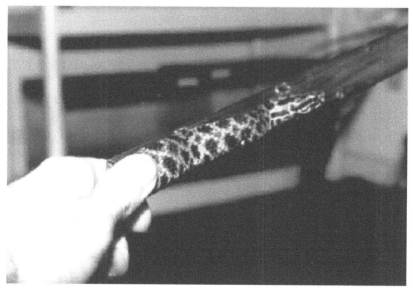

Tubing a Dusky Pygmy Rattlesnake.

In practice, things might not be so simple. Your snake may voluntarily enter the tube and crawl right on in for you. It may not. Some coaxing with a snakestick may be sufficient to get him in. It may not. It is usually easier to get a reluctant snake into a tube if you place it in a large empty bucket or holding bin first. Feeling exposed and vulnerable, the snake will immediately begin looking for a closed-in hiding spot, and if presented with the open end of the snake tube, will often decide that this will do nicely.

Another strategy is to wait until the snake is inside its hide box, and then place the tube over the entrance hole. If the snake wants to come out, he'll need to enter the tube, and then you have him.

You should take care not to put your fingers over any holes in the tube that happen to be near the snake's head. It may be possible for long-fanged snakes to protrude their fangs far enough to reach you through the hole.

Squeeze Box

The squeeze box is an alternative to the tube – although somewhat, in my opinion, less workable. It does provide an easier and safer method of restraining an aggressive snake or a fast and agile elapid than the tube. However, it also presents a greater risk of injury to the snake.

The squeeze box is a wooden container, large enough to hold the coiled snake, with a thick cushion of foam rubber on the floor. A clear plexiglass piece, which fits snugly inside the box, serves as the moveable barrier. When the snake is placed in the squeeze box, the plexiglass barrier is dropped into place and pressed down, squeezing the snake against the foam pad and rendering it immobile. A system of locking screws through the side of the box can be used to hold the barrier in place, freeing both of your hands to do the necessary work.

Care must be taken; too much pressure can severely injure the snake, while not enough pressure will allow the snake to move around.

In order to carry out tasks such as giving injections or removing retained eyecaps, a number of holes, between 1/8 and 3/8 in diameter, should be drilled through the plexiglass barrier. These give access to the snake. A number of retaining screws can be driven through the sides of the box and used to secure the barrier in place, keeping the snake pinned while freeing both hands for work.

While tubing a snake is less stressful and more versatile, squeeze boxes may be a viable alternative when dealing with agile and dangerous snakes that are difficult to tube.

Snake Shields

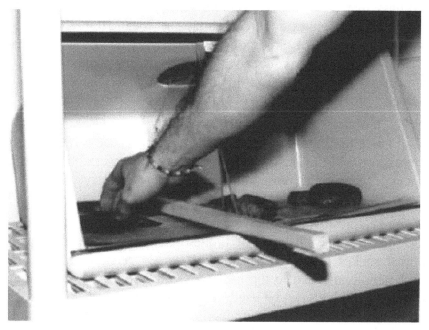

Using the snake shield to change the water in a rattlesnake's cage.

One of the most common causes of bites from captive venomous snakes is the result of both impatience and complacency on the part of the keeper. When in a hurry and faced with the mundane task of changing the water dish or scooping the snake poop yet again, and seeing that the snake is apparently dozing peacefully in a corner, many hot keepers (including those who should know better) yield to temptation, thinking "well, if I'm quick, I can just reach in there and pull the dish out before the snake wakes up". It may even work the first time you try it. But sooner or later you will get zapped, resulting in a quick trip to the hospital. It is indeed surprising how many hot keepers take leave of their senses and voluntarily disregard the prime rule of venomous snake keeping—"Never put any body part within striking range of a hot snake. Ever".

Snake shields are simple pieces of equipment that allow you to perform some routine tasks, such as changing a water bowl or scooping out feces, without the necessity of removing the snake from the cage. The idea is simple: place a transparent impenetrable barrier between you and the snake, and the snake cannot strike you. Some good workable shields can be made inexpensively from pieces of plexiglass that are screwed securely onto wooden handles. A few dollars worth of plastic purchased at the local Home Depot and attached to a couple of old broomsticks will provide you with a handy little tool that greatly reduces your risk of getting tagged. Some of your shields should be "front-mounted" and some should be "side-mounted", and they should be of sufficient size to completely close off one side of the tank or the opening to a hide box.

Once the cage is opened, simply place the see-through barrier between you and the snake, and you can work comfortably while still being able to keep an eye on him should he get aggressive.

Be careful when using shields on fast-moving and agile snakes like large elapids, who might have no problem squeezing under or over your barrier. They also are of limited usefulness when it comes to arboreal snakes (although a somewhat larger version of the shield, with a handle attached to the back that you can grip like a medieval swordsman's shield, can be useful in this situation). Snake shields do work very well with terrestrial viperids. They are my favorite tool to use when it comes to doing routine cage maintenance for my collection of rattlers and copperheads.

Holding Bins

The holding bin is simply a secure escape-proof temporary enclosure where you can place the snake while you are cleaning out its cage or doing other necessary husbandry tasks. Holding bins should be smooth sided and have a lid that can be tightly secured. Some keepers recommend placing a pile of towels or rags in the bottom of the holding bin, to give the snake somewhere to hide and make it less likely to try and zip out while you are putting on the lid. This is not usually necessary for viperids, though, and would only make it more difficult to hook the snake back out of the bin.

For maximum security, try to make the depth of the holding bin at least as deep as the snake is long. Also, try to get a bin that is made of clear plastic to give you a view inside. Taking the lid off a holding bin is a lot safer if you can see where the snake is beforehand, to insure that he's not lurking near the rim, ready to leap out the instant you open it.

For small viperids, I use a plastic storage "sweater box" container with a lid that latches securely at the sides. Larger snakes can be confined in plastic garbage cans with locking lids.

Hooking a rattlesnake into a holding bin.

You should, of course, never leave an occupied holding bin unattended, and should promptly put the snake back in its secure cage as soon as you are done with it.

Forceps

A pair of forceps is a good all-purpose tool for the hot room. These are available from many reptile supply houses in a variety of sizes and shapes. Some look like big tweezers, others look like barbecue tongs, while some are locking hemostats used by surgeons. All are handy for such tasks as placing dead prey animals into the cage or picking out a shed skin or moving the water dish. (Be sure to use a snake shield while doing this.) Forceps should be long enough to keep your hand out of the snake's strike radius.

Some keepers also like to use a long metal spoon for scooping snake poop out of the substrate. Since I use newspaper in all my cages, I don't use the spoon method, but it might be useful if you use aspen chips or bark nuggets in your cages.

Catchboxes

A good catchbox should be a standard bit of equipment for every hot snake keeper. In the case of large and aggressive vipers or agile and dangerous elapids, they are an absolute necessity. Properly utilized, a catchbox (also known as a shift box, a trapbox or a capture box) makes it possible to secure even the most lethal of snakes while greatly reducing the level of risk to the keeper. Catchboxes are a far safer alternative than any of the other handling methods discussed so far.

A catchbox is, basically, a standard wooden or plastic hide box with a moveable plexiglass door that can be slid over the entrance hole using a snakestick, and then securely fastened to confine the snake inside. As long as the door is secure and the box cannot be penetrated by fangs, you can transport the snake in complete safety. Similar systems are used by zoos to safely confine dangerous snakes like king cobras and taipans so the cages can be cleaned and maintained. It is a good idea to have two catchboxes for each snake, so one can be cleaned while the other is in use.

Since no catchboxes are commercially available, you will have to make your own. The catchbox should be the same size that you would use as a hide box for the snake. A box measuring 9 inches long, 5 inches wide and 3 inches deep is suitable for snakes up to around 2 ft in length, while a 12 x 6 x 4 inch box can comfortably secure all but the largest vipers or elapids.

The simplest catchboxes are made from ½ inch plywood. Simply nail together a box of the appropriate size, making sure there are no gaps or openings anywhere along the edges. The lid must fit absolutely securely (it's a good idea to use a rubber or foam padded gasket around the rim of the box to seal off any potential gaps). The lid should be hinged at the back and have a hasp arrangement at the front that can accept a padlock, allowing you to securely lock the snake in. This allows you to open the lid and remove the snake from the catchbox, using a hook or tongs, if this should become necessary (for extra security, make the hasp large enough that you can operate it with a snake hook instead of your fingers). The lid also allows you to clean out feces and any other mess that the snake may leave inside the box.

If you will be using the catchbox to transport the snake or to confine it for a long period of time (perhaps for use in educational shows), you will need to drill a few small ventilation holes in the sides or top (do not place your fingers over these when handling the box).

Drill an entrance hole in the front just wide enough for the snake to squeeze through. The plexiglass door is made large enough to completely cover the entrance hole, with some comfortable overlap. It fits into a wooden frame at the front of the box, and is held in place by slats of wood that overlap the door enough to secure it while still allowing it to slide back and forth. Place a screw with a wide head (a small eyescrew is also suitable) through the plexi at the side edge to serve as a handle, and insert a similar screw in the wooden frame on the same side. When the door is closed, these two screws should lie next to each other, where they can be securely wired together to secure the door.

When it becomes necessary to work inside the cage, wait until the snake is safely inside the hide box (you may perhaps use a snakestick on some of the slower-moving species to "herd" it into the box) and use your snakestick to slide the door shut. Lift the box out and secure the door with wire. When you are finished with the cage, return the catchbox, unfasten the door, and use the snakestick to open it. Since the snake is securely hidden in its usual hiding spot, it suffers far less stress and anxiety than it would if it were hooked or tonged out into the open. The catchbox system allows you to deal with even the most lethal of snakes without exposing yourself to any potential bites. It is by far the safest method of moving a venomous snake.

Some modifications made during the construction of your catchbox can add to its versatility (and your safety). One option is to add a removable plexiglass barrier to the inside top of the box, with a number of small retaining screws inserted through the side of the box to hold it in place. This allows you to safely give a close visual inspection to dangerously aggressive snakes that would otherwise be difficult to pin or tube. If you place a foam rubber pad at the bottom of the box, you can convert the catchbox into a "squeeze box" by pressing the snake between the moveable plexiglass barrier and the padding to immobilize it. If you further modify the barrier by drilling a number of holes through it, you can use these to perform medical tasks upon the immobilized snake in much the same way as you would with a tube (a second set of retaining screws can be installed to hold the barrier securely in place while the snake is thus immobilized).

Bagging Methods

With the exception of using a catchbox, bagging is the most secure and safest method of confining and transporting a venomous snake. It is also the method of choice for use in capturing hot snakes in the field. Every hot snake keeper must be well practiced in the various methods of safely bagging a venomous snake.

Although there are special-purpose snake bags available commercially, most snake keepers use ordinary pillow cases, since these are readily available and inexpensive. These must be modified somewhat before they can be used. The inside seam must be carefully checked, particularly at the corners, to make sure there are no weak spots or holes that could serve as potential escape routes. I like to go over all the seams of my new snake bags with a sewing machine, just to reinforce them. Finally, the snake bag will be much safer to use if you sew a small loop of material to each corner, both top and bottom.

Custom-made snake bags in different sizes are not difficult to make. Simply take a piece of cloth the same length and twice as wide as the finished size you want, fold it in half and double-sew the edges using a sewing machine. Be sure to carefully inspect the seams for any gaps or loose areas. Then turn it inside out, so the seams are on the inside, and add the loops to the outside corners. Lighter cloth is easier to tie and work with than is heavier stiffer material, and I have found that dark-colored bags make the confined snakes feel more secure and calm than white ones do.

The size of the bag will vary according to the size of the snake to be placed in it. For the small (1.5 - 3 feet) terrestrial viperids that I usually work with, I use custom-made snake bags that are 14 inches wide and about 28 inches long. Standard pillow cases, measuring 20 inches wide and 30 inches long, can be used to confine snakes up to about 6 feet in length, and custom-made larger bags can be used for longer snakes. For maximum safety when bagging agile or aggressive snakes like elapids, try to use a bag that is at least as deep as the snake is long.

Bagging Bucket

An ordinary plastic bucket or wastepaper basket can serve for use in the field or in the snake room. The bucket should have the same diameter as the snake bag you will be using, and should be three or four inches shorter than the length of the bag.

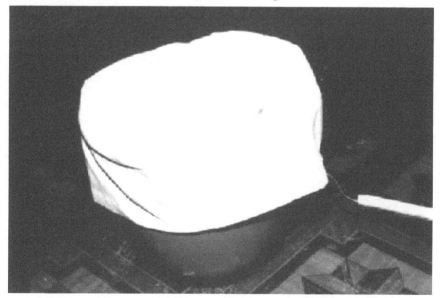

To bag a snake, set up the bucket by placing the bag inside and then wrapping the edge so it overlaps the rim of the bucket by about three inches.

Check to insure that the bag is firmly in place and cannot be pulled loose, then thread the hook of a snakestick through the loop at the upper corner of the bag to act as a handle.

Using another snakestick, pick up the snake and place it in the bag, then pull the bag closed at one side and lay the stick across the bag to hold it closed and prevent the snake from squeezing underneath.

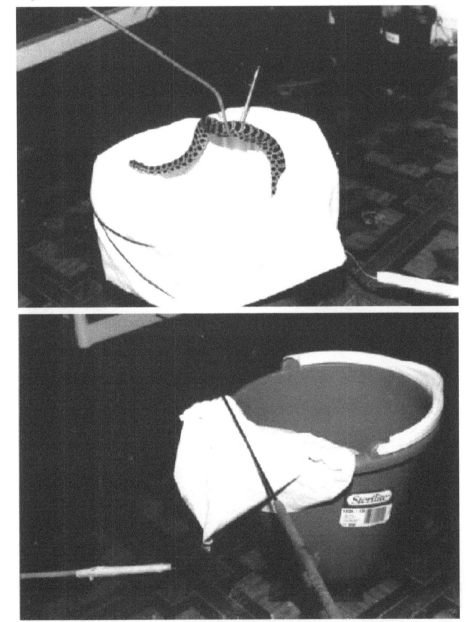

Now, you can safely twist the bag closed and tie an overhand knot to seal it. Once tied, the bag can be safely carried above the knot.

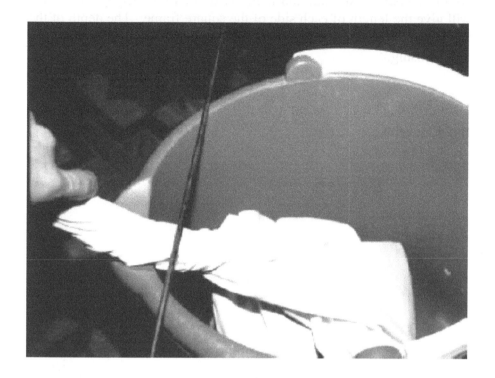

Do not allow the bag to touch any part of your body, since most hot snakes are fully capable of biting through the cloth. Bagged snakes should always be placed inside plastic buckets or wooden boxes for extra safety, and this container should always be clearly labeled "Live Venomous Snakes".

Bagging Frame

A more permanent version of the bagging bucket, for use in the snake room, uses a wooden frame instead of a bucket. The bagging frame consists of a wooden framework, securely fastened to the floor, that is used to hold open a bag while the snake is being placed within. The size of the frame will depend on the size of the bag you will be using, and if your collection consists of several differently-sized snakes, you will need a range of frame and bag sizes as well.

Most of the frames I have seen are four-sided and square in configuration. To calculate the size frame you will need, measure the width of your snake bag, and then divide this number by two. This will give the length of each side of the square frame. The depth of the frame should be three or four inches less than the length of the bag you will be using.

Bagging Stick

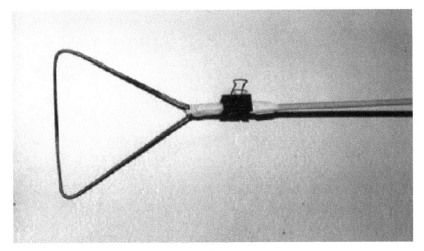

The bagging stick is a versatile tool.

A purpose-built bagging stick, which can be used in the field or in the snake room, is the most versatile and easiest-to-use method of bagging a venomous snake. The bagging stick consists of a metal frame mounted at the end of a stick. The only commercially available versions of this handy little device that I have seen have round frames, but all the ones I have made myself are triangular in shape, which, I believe, gives a better grip and is more secure. The disadvantage of the triangular frame, though, is that it makes the opening of the bag somewhat smaller, which can make bagging agile snakes somewhat more difficult.

For the small rattlesnakes and copperheads that I keep, I use a triangular bagging frame, a little over 9 inches on a side, that I bent from 3/8 inch steel rod. This is attached to a 36-inch wooden dowel that serves as a handle. I use a spring clip, such as those found on clipboards, to secure the bag to the frame.

To load the bagging stick, pull the snake bag up through the hoop from the bottom, overlapping the edge of the frame by about three inches. Pull the rear edge of the bag tightly against the handle, and pin it in place using the spring clip. Pull sharply on the bottom of the bag to make sure it is securely in place. The bagging stick is now ready for use.

Hold the bagging stick firmly in your left hand, or have a partner hold it for you. With your right hand, use a snakestick to place the snake into the bag.

Then allow the weight of the snake to rest on the floor, place the front edge of the triangular frame on the floor (taking care not to pin the snake's head or body underneath it) and pull up sharply on the handle towards the rear of the bag, to fold the edge of the bag against the straight edge of the frame, sealing it off. The opening of the bag should now be facing away from you, and the triangular frame should be pressing against the floor, preventing the snake from escaping.

Quickly lay a snakestick across the opening (place your foot on the shaft) to prevent the snake from working his way out, then twist the bag closed by making a circular motion with the handle of the bagging stick.

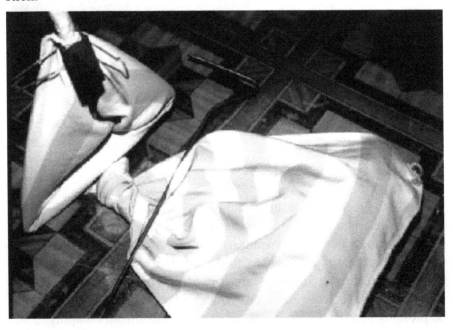

Once it is securely closed, you can safely tie an overhand knot in the bag to confine the snake.

I prefer the bagging stick over either the frame or the bucket, since the stick can be hung on the wall when it is not in use, where it is out of the way and doesn't clutter up the floor like a frame or bucket does.

Un-Bagging a Snake

Removing a venomous snake from a bag should be done with the same care and caution that was used to put him in. Keep in mind that a hot snake is fully capable of biting through a closed bag.

To safely un-bag a snake, lay the bag on the floor and place a snakestick across the neck of the bag, as far below the knot as you can without pinning the snake. Place your foot on the shaft to hold the stick in place, pressing it against the floor and firmly sealing off the opening.

Now you are free to untie the knot and unwind the neck of the bag.

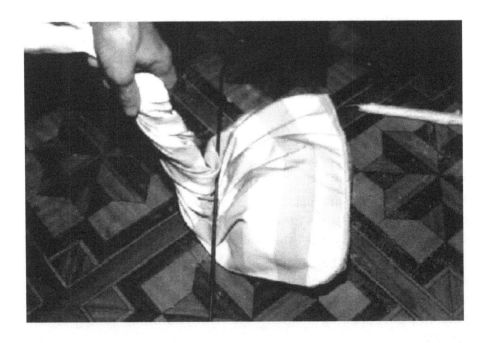

Place the hook of a second snakestick through the loop at the bottom corner of the bag, remove the first snakestick from the bag, and gently tip the snake out.

If necessary, once the snake is out of the bag, use your snakestick to move him to his cage.

Types of Snakes

In terms of size and handling characteristics, most venomous snakes fall into one of six categories. These are what I call the "ankle biters", the "head hunters", the "knee nippers", the "gotchas", the "racers" and the "mad dogs". While some species vary widely in behavior, and even individual snakes will change their "mood" from day to day, these categories can serve as a rough rule of thumb.

Ankle Biters—The "ankle biters" present the lowest level of danger. This category consists of the small terrestrial snakes, up to 2.5 or 3 feet in body length, like the pygmy rattlers, copperheads, and European adders. With a strike range of less than a foot, and a pretty good tendency to stay on stick, these little guys are the easiest of all the hot snakes to handle. Most of them are not capable of injecting a lethal dose, so although a bite will cause a lot of pain and tremendous local tissue damage, you probably won't die from your mistake. The "ankle biters" make good snakes for new hot keepers to learn the ropes on (my first venomous snake was a young Northern Copperhead).

Southern Copperhead

Young individuals of most other viperids can also be treated like ankle biters, although the venom may pack more of a punch. A few of the small "ankle biters", such as the tiny saw-scaled viper, or the coral snakes, have very dangerous venom and should be only kept by experienced keepers.

Head Hunters—The "head hunters"---the small arboreal vipers like eyelash vipers, bush vipers and the various snakes of the *Trimeresurus* genus—present an increased level of danger from the "ankle biters", and are for more experienced hot keepers.

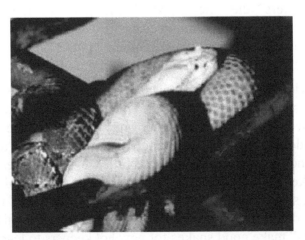

Eyelash Viper

Most of the arboreal vipers are irrascible little guys and not particularly friendly, striking at anything that approaches their perch. They can also be deceptive—although they are short little tykes, they can hang on with their tails and reach out virtually the entire length of their body to get you, which may surprise unwary keepers. And since many of them make their living by snagging birds in mid-air as they fly by, their reflexes are incredible and their strike is fast and accurate. Being arboreal, they also tend to be at head height, and often strike at your face. The good news is that most of them are sub-lethal. Be very careful around these guys.

Because the arboreal vipers can be very delicate and very demanding in their environmental conditions, I don't recommend them for beginning hot keepers. Save them until you are more comfortable with the basic equipment and procedures, and can focus more on husbandry issues.

Knee Nippers—Most of the mid-size terrestrial vipers in the 3 to 6 ft range fall into this category, including the rattlesnakes, the pit vipers and the true vipers. Although their habits and lifestyles are similar to those of the little "ankle biters", the larger size, longer reach and more potent venom of the "knee nippers" makes them more dangerous and more difficult to handle. These snakes are only for experienced keepers.

Timber Rattlesnake

The good news is that most of the mid-size viperids aren't very difficult to handle. They don't usually object to being handled with a snakestick, as long as you are careful to stay out of their strike radius. A catchbox is, of course, much safer. I make it a practice to always wear snake-proof boots when working with any of the "knee nippers".

Gotchas—The "gotchas" are very deceptive snakes, and very very dangerous. Big and fat and lazy-looking, they will often spend days at a time curled up in a corner, unmoving. When they do amble around, they are slow, plodding and dignified. Inexperienced keepers may be forgiven for thinking that these big fat sausages wouldn't even have the energy to try and strike.

Gaboon Viper

Nevertheless, these snakes are like living bear traps. If you are ever so foolish as to stick your hand in their tank, these snakes may at first not even move an inch. You may perhaps see a very slight movement of the eyes, or an ever so imperceptible increase in the breathing rate. Then----***POW***!!! Before you even know what has happened, the snake has both fangs in you, and you are on your way to the hospital.

Snakes that fall into the "gotcha" category are the Gaboon and rhinoceros vipers, the puff adders, and the other snakes of the *Bitis* genus. Some of the big heavy rattlesnakes and large adult cottonmouths with a body length of more than 5 feet can also sometimes act like "gotchas".

What makes the "gotchas" so dangerous? These snakes have evolved to be "ambush predators". When they are hungry, they simply curl their big fat bodies up in a likely spot and wait, unmoving, for days. When something wanders by, the snake focuses all its senses on it, but doesn't move a muscle, to avoid scaring off the prey until it gets closer. When the prey moves within striking range, the trap is sprung. *Pow.*

These snakes can strike in virtually any direction from virtually any body position, and their strike is instant, powerful and unerringly accurate. Big vipers like this have been known to shatter the glass at the front of their enclosures by striking at it. I've seen puff adders that were sprawled lazily on the floor strike accurately at a snakestick that was two feet directly behind their tail, turning over in mid-air to do it. They also have the longest fangs of any venomous snakes, and a very powerful venom. Don't underestimate these guys. They are killers.

Although it is possible to tail a big Gaboon or cottonmouth, this is extremely hazardous, and I don't recommend you try it. They are very powerful snakes, and if it comes to a flat-out wrestling match, you will lose. Play it safe. Use a catchbox, and don't ever let any portion of your anatomy get within the strike radius of one of these snakes. Ever.

Racers—The contrast between the "gotchas" and the "racers" could not be more vivid. While the "gotchas" are so slow and lazy that you might need to check them occasionally to see if they are still breathing, the "racers" are agile, quick and seemingly never sit still for ten seconds. The "racers" include the cobras and nearly all the other elapids. Most of the rear-fanged colubrids, like boomslangs, twig snakes and flying snakes, are also "racers", and some of the agile viperids, like the lance-headed pit vipers from South America, can be just as "runny".

Handling the "racers" can be pure hell. They zip across the floor at top speed, are nearly impossible to get on a hook, refuse to stay on stick (or worse, try to climb up the stick towards you), and even getting them into a tube can be a real workout. They are also nervous and get spooked easily.

Monocled Cobra

The good news is that the strike of a cobra or other elapid isn't as fast as that of a viperid, and since they usually make a few half-hearted "threat strikes" in your direction first, you can usually see it coming. Given the chance, these snakes will retreat rather than bite.

Some of the "racers" will stay relatively still if they are picked up on two snakesticks, but I wouldn't count on it. They can be tailed more easily than the big viperids can be, but tailing a big cobra is a hazardous undertaking. Use tongs on them if you begin losing control. But your best bet is to use your catchbox religiously.

Me? I prefer not to mess with any of the elapids.

Mad Dogs—The "mad dogs" include the black mambas, king cobras, and the taipans. These elapids are every bit as fast and agile as the "racers" and every bit as difficult to control, with the added complication that these snakes (some of them are the most lethal animals on the planet) will not hesitate to turn and advance on you with the express intention of poking holes somewhere in your body. It's hard enough chasing a big elapid around on the floor, without the added fun of having the snake attempt to chase *you* too.

King Cobra

Another group that must be added to this category are the spitting cobras. Not fun to work with. Wear an eyeshield (diver's goggles work well, as do clear welders-type masks) and be damn careful.

Why do I call these snakes "mad dogs"? First, because they can attack with all the ferocity of a rabid pit bull. Second, because only mad dogs and Englishmen would be dumb enough to try to keep one.

Catchbox. Enough said.

Learn From These Mistakes

Here is where I begin to drive home the lessons from real life. Throughout this website, I have emphasized that hot snake keeping is serious business, with serious potential consequences. Now you will begin to see why.

Let's start with some of the flubs and goof-ups that I've heard about. Some of these were made by newbie keepers. Others come from people with years of experience. All of them show how easy it is to suffer from a momentary lapse. Learn from *these* mistakes, and hopefully you won't need to learn from your *own*. The hard way.

Let's begin with a keeper of my acquaintance. He had an adult pygmy rattler that he kept for a long time. It was docile, never rattled, rarely struck and was, as my friend says, "like a corn snake". One day, my friend saw that the snake's water bowl needed changing, and seeing the snake curled up placidly in a corner, decided that he'd be able to reach in there, pull the water bowl out, and his nice friendly snake would be none the wiser.

Zap.

Lesson learned: Trust no one. Even the most docile and placid snake can have a bad day, and you'll never know when that will be. Don't ever get complacent with any hot snake. Another lesson: remember the Prime Directive. Never put any part of your body within the strike range of a hot snake.

Western Diamondback Rattlesnake

Another keeper had a large prairie rattlesnake. One day, he decided to take it out and show it off to his new girlfriend. While the snake sat coiled up on the floor, Mr Macho decided to show his new love how fast the rattler can strike, and casually poked his foot towards its face. The snake promptly bit him in the ankle.

Lessons learned: Forget all the stupid macho hot-dogging and showing off. It'll only get you killed one day. The best and most long-lived hot keepers are the ones who take the fewest chances. Another lesson: never involve an inexperienced person with an unconfined hot snake. Mr Macho was able to put the snake back in its cage before carting himself off to the hospital. If Mr Macho had collapsed on the floor instead, Miss Perfect wouldn't have been able to do anything except stand there and scream, and very likely would have become Victim Number Two in short order.

At a party, some reptile keepers were relaxing around some hot snake cages when one of them casually leaned back and put his arm on top of a nearby cage. The occupant promptly bit him through the screen at the top of the tank.

Lessons learned: Situational awareness. You must always be aware of your surroundings and always keep in mind any potential trouble spots. Another lesson: secure well-designed caging is worth its weight in gold.

Eastern Diamondback Rattlesnake

An inexperienced keeper tried to feed his new eyelash viper by offering it a dead mouse on a pair of tongs, and was bitten in the wrist.

Lessons learned: Know your snakes. When dealing with a new species, know all its idiosyncracies. Had this newbie known that arboreal vipers have an extraordinarily long reach, he wouldn't have gotten tagged. Another lesson: don't underestimate the strike range of a hot snake. More than one person has been tagged because he "thought the snake can't reach this far". The big *Bitis* vipers are particularly dangerous in this capacity, since they can strike in virtually any direction and can easily catch an inexperienced keeper by surprise.

From Australia. While wandering home from the bar one night, a man found a large king brown snake crossing the road and decided to capture it. Since he was holding his beer can in his right hand, he decided to pick it up with his left hand, and was promptly bitten. After getting the snake into a bucket, he wanted to take a closer look and was bitten again. He survived, but lost his arm.

Lessons learned (*sigh*—this'll be a long list); Alcohol and snakes don't mix. If you insist on handling snakes when you're crocked, you are asking for big trouble. Another lesson: know your limits. A newbie like this messing around with a dangerous and agile snake like the king brown is just begging to get killed. If you don't know what you're doing, don't do it. And another lesson: use the proper tools. That's what they are there for.

An experienced herpetologist was attempting to handle a boomslang to examine it for an identification, and pinned it and picked it up. His grip was too far back on the neck, allowing the snake to turn and sink a fang into his finger.

Lesson learned: Silly mistakes like this can happen at any time. If they happen once too often, you are dead. Another lesson: pinning a snake, no matter how many times you've done it before, is a hazardous and risky operation. Don't do it unless there is no other alternative.

An experienced cobra breeder was in a hurry and had to do some cage maintenance tasks. In his haste he slipped up and was bitten. Fortunately for him, it turned out to be a dry bite.

Lesson learned: Keep your wits sharp. Anything that distracts you for even an instant is a potential danger.

Snakebite: If You Goof Up

Of the 2700 known species of snakes, only about 400 possess fangs and a venom apparatus, and of these, only about 200 are known to be dangerous to humans. Snakebite is an extremely rare occurrence in industrialized nations. Most emergency room doctors go their entire careers without ever seeing a snakebite case. Because most venomous snakes require unaltered natural habitat, the chances are not good that they will ever encounter a human in the wild.

Venomous snake keepers, of course, increase the odds of a bite tremendously, by being near and interacting with venomous snakes on a daily basis. Although many venomous snake keepers go their whole lives without a bite (I've never been bitten—yet), many eventually get tagged. If you do get a bite, the chances are very good that the emergency room doctors who examine you will never have seen a snakebite case before, and their knowledge and experience in these matters will be limited at best. If you are going to be keeping venomous snakes, then, it is in your best interests to know what happens during a snakebite and why. It is also a good idea to meet with the doctors at the local emergency room, to make sure that they know you will be keeping venomous snakes and may need treatment for a bite, and to insure that they are prepared for that eventuality.

Snake venom is a mixture of proteins that are manufactured and stored in the snake's venom glands until needed. In appearance, venom is a pale yellow liquid. The viperids have long fangs that fold up against the roof of the mouth when not in use. The elapids, like cobras and coral snakes, have short fixed fangs that remain erect. In both cases, the fangs are located at the front of the mouth, and are connected to the venom glands in the cheeks by a short duct. When the snake bites, muscles in the head squeeze the venom glands, forcing venom through the duct and out the end of the hollow fangs into the victim. These muscles are under the conscious control of the snake, allowing it to precisely control the amount of venom it injects with each bite.

Even a mildly venomous snake, like this Northern Copperhead, can be dangerous if you happen to be allergic to the venom.

In the rear-fanged snakes, such as the boomslang and the twig snake, the venom injection apparatus is different from the vipers and the elapids—it is designed to inject venom only after the snake's prey has already been partially swallowed. There are often three or four fangs on each side of the head, located at the rear of the upper jaw. Pressure on the jawbones causes the Duvernoy's glands to ooze venom, which then dribbles down grooves on the side of the fangs to enter the victim's flesh. Because this system is rather inefficient, rear-fanged snakes that bite humans often hang on to their victim, chewing it repeatedly to work the venom into the bite wound.

The primary purpose of snake venom is to obtain and pre-digest the animal's food. Its defensive uses are secondary.

Because of its importance to its survival, snakes will take steps to conserve their precious venom. Very often, a hot snake that strikes in self-defense will not inject any venom, a phenomenon known as a "dry bite". In pit vipers, between one-third and one-half of all defensive bites are dry. In elapids, the percentage is even higher, between one-half and two-thirds. Rear-fanged snakes are not capable of controlling the amount of venom they inject, and are not capable of inflicting dry bites. However, because the fangs are so far back in the mouth, it is also difficult for rear-fanged snakes to inject a lot of venom.

In most cases where the snake actually does inject venom, the amount injected is so small that no clinical symptoms result. Fewer than 5% of snake bites actually result in severe envenomation. And even in severe envenomations, death in humans is rare. The death rate for untreated snakebites varies from zero to fifty percent (the average is about fifteen percent), depending on such factors as the species involved, the size and health of the victim, and the circumstances of the bite.

Over 30 different proteins and enzymes have been found in snake venoms. Several dozen more have not yet been scientifically described. Each has a particular function, and often attacks a particular body organ or structure. All are quickly carried through the body in the lymphatic system and in the bloodstream. Proteolysins act to break down cell walls. Hemorrhagins dissolve the walls of capillaries and blood vessels to cause massive internal bleeding. Cardiotoxins attack the muscles of the heart. Cytolysins attack and kill white blood cells. Phospholipase fractions attack the nerve cells. Hyaluronidase attacks the connective tissues, breaking them apart and allowing the other venom fractions to enter the tissues deeply. Polypeptides attack the production of acetylcholine, interfering with nerve functions. Hemolysins attack and break apart the red blood cells. Thrombinases remove the blood's ability to clot.

Snake venoms can be divided into two major categories, although elements of one are always found in the other. Hemotoxic venom contains a high proportion of hemorrhagins and proteolysins. These venoms work by breaking down the victim's body tissues, destroying cell walls and blood vessels and producing massive internal bleeding. Death usually results from internal bleeding and a severe drop in blood pressure. Neurotoxic venoms, in contrast, produce little tissue damage, but contain a high proportion of phospholipases and polypeptides, and attack the transfer of nerve impulses by interfering with the actions of cholinesterase and acetylcholine. The victim becomes numb as the nerves become progressively disabled. Death results when the nerves that power the diaphragm are shut off, paralyzing the muscle and causing the victim to suffocate.

In general, the viperids tend to have venom that is strongly hemotoxic, while the elapids tend to have venom that is more strongly neurotoxic. This is not a hard and fast rule, however. Elements of both are often found in all snakes. The death adder, an Australian elapid, has venom that is strongly hemotoxic, while the Mojave rattlesnake and the South American cascabel, both viperids, have strongly neurotoxic venom. There are indications that the venom mix of timber rattlesnakes and eastern diamondbacks in the southern United States are changing, becoming more strongly neurotoxic.

Symptoms from neurotoxic and hemotoxic envenomations are very different. In a neurotoxic bite, there may be very little initial pain from the short fangs, and because there is little local tissue destruction, there is not usually much swelling or discoloration either. It is not unusual for victims of neurotoxic snakebite to not feel any symptoms at all for one to eight hours after the bite. During the initial moments after the venom was injected, however, the polypeptides and phospholipases have already travelled quickly through the body and bound themselves to the cells of the cranial nerves, where they begin their work.

Within an hour of a severe bite, the victim will begin to feel a tingling sensation in his fingers and scalp. This is followed by a headache, drowsiness, a feeling of euphoria or "dreaminess", slurred speech, and often nausea and vomiting. As the sensation of numbness increases, the heart rate will increase significantly, and the limbs become heavy and difficult to move as paralysis begins. Breathing becomes difficult, and the victim feels as if there is a heavy weight on his chest. Death results if the diaphragm becomes paralyzed. The timing of this sequence depends on the severity of the bite.

Usually, even in severe bites, there may not be any symptoms at all for over an hour. Mild envenomations may experience only the earliest symptoms, and only hours after the bite. More severe bites can produce the full sequence within an hour of the bite, over a period of three or four hours. In rare cases, such as direct injection of the venom into an artery, the entire suite of symptoms occurs within minutes and death is almost immediate.

The symptoms of an envenomation by a hemotoxic snake, by contrast, are severe, immediate and unmistakable. Within seconds of the bite, there will be a sharp burning pain in the affected area. Within one minute, swelling and discoloration will begin as the snake proteins start to break down the surrounding tissues.

Within ten minutes, the swelling and bruising will be unmistakable, and the pain will be severe. This is often accompanied by severe and violent vomiting. Within half an hour, most of the affected limb will be swollen and black and blue as the underlying tissues are digested away. Blood blisters may form, and the affected areas may crack open and bleed.

The pain and tenderness will be so severe than even the touch of clothing on the limb produces agony. There may also be a feeling of weakness or light-headedness, and a rapid but weak pulse.

In severe cases, blood may drain from the nose, kidneys and intestines. Within 24 hours of the bite, the limb will be swollen to twice its normal size.

The time of onset of these symptoms can be taken as a rough indication of the severity of the bite. The more venom has been injected, the more rapidly the swelling and bruising will progress. Because of the tremendous local tissue destruction, it is not unusual, in severe bites, for amputation of the affected digit to become necessary.

What should you do if you are bitten? Forget everything you've ever heard about cutting and sucking out the venom. Forget about using electric shocks from a stun gun, or packing the bitten limb in ice. Forget about tourniquets or constriction bands. None of these "treatments" work, and they all do more harm than good. The only first aid measure that can be effective is the use of a "Sawyer extractor", a device that sucks envenomed fluids out through the fang punctures themselves. The Sawyer extractor, however, is only effective if used within seconds of the bite. After that, the venoms have already traveled too far into the body's tissues to be removed.

There is a well-respected saying among venomous snake keepers----"The best equipment for treating a venomous snake bite is a set of car keys". Back when we were discussing the setup of the hot snake room, we decided to place a telephone and a spare set of car keys on one wall. Here's why. If you are bitten by any sort of venomous snake, confine the snake so it can't bite anyone else, take off any jewelry such as rings or bracelets that might become trapped if the limb begins swelling, go immediately to the phone, tell the hospital you're on the way, then get yourself in the car and get to the emergency room as fast as you are able. Do not delay, even if you are not feeling any symptoms yet. This is especially important with neurotoxic snakes that might not produce any symptoms at first. As I was writing this chapter, a snake keeper in Florida was bitten by his cobra and, not feeling any initial symptoms, decided it was a dry bite and didn't go to the hospital. An hour later, he was struck by a wave of paralysis and was dead within minutes.

If the hospital is more than an hour away, you can use the "Australia method" of first aid, to help slow the onset of symptoms until you can reach medical help. Developed for use against the deadly Australian elapids, this process consists of wrapping the entire affected limb firmly with an Ace bandage or other elastic strip, and immobilizing the limb with a splint. The idea here is not to cut off or impede blood flow, but to slow the movement of lymph and thus help delay the spread of the venom until medical help is available.

The only effective treatment for a venomous snakebite is the use of antivenom, sometimes referred to as antivenin. Antivenoms are produced by injecting a horse with small amounts of venom, which causes the horse's body to produce antibodies that can neutralize the toxins. Over time, the horse's blood contains enough antibodies to neutralize even a lethal dose of venom. At that point, the horse blood is extracted and the serum portion is purified and sterilized to form antivenom.

Antivenoms are only effective against the particular venoms that were used to produce them, although many laboratories produce "polyvalent" antivenoms by exposing the horse to a number of different venoms at the same time, allowing the animal to develop resistance to them all. In the United States, a single polyvalent antivenom is available that treats all of the North American pit vipers. A separate antivenom is used for coral snake bites.

Florida Cottonmouth

If you are keeping any non-native species of venomous snake, you will need to insure that your local hospital has an adequate supply (at least 25 vials) of antivenom for that particular species. Antivenom for foreign snakes can run over $1,000 a vial. Consider it an investment.

In any snakebite case where systemic symptoms appear, the doctor will probably introduce at least five vials of antivenom right away, using an IV drip, and then one or two vials per hour until improvement. A severe bite may require as many as 20 vials. Antivenom is most effective if given within three hours of the bite.

It is very likely that the emergency room doctor will have never had to use a snakebite antivenom before, so you will want him to consult with an experienced person during the treatment. This is particularly important if you have been bitten by an exotic non-native species, since all of the available antivenoms for foreign species are unregulated and unapproved by the FDA, and your doctor may be reluctant and unsure how to use them. (You can expect to sign all sorts of forms waiving liability for the hospital and doctor.) Have your physician contact the local Poison Control Center for a list of available resources and consultants. The Jacobi Hospital in Bronx, New York, also has an emergency hotline for information and consulting on exotic and native snakebites.

One potential problem with snakebite antivenom is that of anaphylactic shock. Since horse serum is also used to produce such common shots as vaccines, many people have already been exposed to the horse proteins. In a small percentage of people, this exposure may be enough to sensitize the body and provoke a severe allergic reaction to any subsequent exposures. Anaphylactic shock is itself life-threatening. Fortunately, a simple skin test before the antivenom is administered will tell the doctor if you are allergic, allowing him to be prepared to treat the allergic reaction with epinephrine. If the bite is severe enough, you will get antivenom even if you are allergic to it.

People who have been bitten by a venomous snake before, or who have been exposed to snake venoms in some other way, are also at an increased risk to allergy or sensitivity in the future, this time to the venom itself. Even a mild bite can sensitize the body to snake proteins, provoking a more severe reaction in any subsequent bites. If you talk to an experienced snaker who has been bitten several times, you will often find that the second or third bites were much worse than the first.

Keep in mind too that exposure to antivenom after a snakebite can also sensitize the body to horse serum, increasing the risk of an allergic response to the antivenom after any subsequent bites.

If you know you are at risk from an anaphylactic shock, through previous exposure to either venom or antivenom, make sure that all the paramedics, nurses and emergency room doctors are aware of that. If you already know that you are allergic to snake venom, it's a good idea to discuss this with your doctor. Allergic reactions can often be lessened by an injection of epinephrin using a device called an Epi-Pen (these devices are routinely carried by people who are allergic to bee stings). In the case of a known allergy, an injection of two Epi-Pens, ten minutes apart, as soon as allergic symptoms appear, can help alleviate the problem.

Even after you have recovered from the snakebite and have not had an allergic reaction to the antivenom, you are still in for a rough time. A large number of people who are treated with antivenom suffer a short time after from an affliction known as "serum sickness". This can appear anywhere from five to twenty-five days after the administration of antivenom. Serum sickness results when the molecular remnants of the destroyed venom begin to lodge in the inner walls of the blood vessels, temporarily restricting blood flow. The symptoms include flu-like fever, lethargy, nausea and vomiting, an itchy rash, swelling and sometimes kidney problems. The larger the dose of antivenom that you received, the more likely you are to experience serum sickness afterwards.

Conclusion

Quite frankly, many people who are keeping venomous snakes, should not be. Many people who keep hot snakes do it for all the wrong reasons, and shouldn't have one to begin with. For too many, their motivation is simple—they want to show off and demonstrate to everyone what a bad-ass they are. Unfortunately, those are the very sort of people who usually get themselves killed, and provoke all sorts of laws and regulations that only make things more difficult for the legitimate, responsible keepers.

Every time some unprepared dolt gets himself bitten by his pet hot snake, it is a crushing blow for those of us in the hobby who are responsible about it. Many times, it leads not only to laws banning the keeping of venomous snakes, but to banning the keeping of *all* snakes, even harmless corn snakes. That is why it is so vitally necessary for snake keepers to use their heads and act responsibly. The trouble that you might cause through irresponsible actions will not reflect just on yourself—it falls on *all* of us.

Lightning Source UK Ltd.
Milton Keynes UK
UKHW02f0830100918
328635UK00012B/573/P